AMERICAN LANDMARKS

The Lighthouse

AMY HANDY

NEW LINE BOOKS

DEDICATION
For my parents, Rose and Lawrence Feldhun, in remembrance of that first visit to Montauk Lighthouse

ACKNOWLEDGEMENTS
I am grateful to my editor, Ann Kirby, for her encouragement and understanding.
Thanks also to Jean Perla, for her road-trip companionship and ever-brewing pots of coffee.
Gratitude also goes to my husband, Christopher, and daughter, Julia, for their love and support.

Fax: (888) 719-7723
E-mail: info@newlinebooks.com

Printed and bound in China

ISBN 978-1-59764-106-7

Visit us on the web!
www.newlinebooks.com

Author: Amy Handy

Publisher: Robert M. Tod
Editorial Director: Elizabeth Loonan
Senior Editor: Cynthia Sternau
Project Editor: Ann Kirby
Photo Editor: Edward Douglas
Picture Researchers: Heather Weigel, Laura Wyss
Production Coordinator: Annie Kaufmann
Design: Theresa Izzillo

PICTURE CREDITS

Albany Institute of History and art 91 (top)
Tom Algire 25, 28-29, 62-63
Charles Braswell, Jr. 17, 22-23, 30, 31 (top),
  46 (bottom)
Bridgeman Art Library 74 (top), 91 (bottom), 96-97
Cincinnati Art Museum, Gift of Alice Scarborough 18
Corbis-Bettmann 13, 16, 24, 35, 39, 46 (top), 57
(top), 60, 70 (bottom), 78 (top), 82, 88 (bottom),
  113 (right)
Dembinsky Photo Associates
Willard Clay 36-37
Dan Dempster 33, 68-69
Ken Scott 94
Dick Dietrich 72-73, 81
Don Eastman 70
John Elk III 102 (bottom), 116 (left)
Esto Photographics 88 (top)
Mary Evans Picture Library 54
Robert Wilson Fagan 40, 77
Dennis Frates 14, 84, 98 (top)
Justine Hill 34
Warren Kimble 113
John and Ann Mahan 59, 64 (top), 83, 86-87, 89,
  92-93, 96 (top), 100-101, 103, 105

Patti McConville and Les Sumner 117
Metropolitan Museum of Art, New York, Kastor Fund,
  1962 (62.95) 51
Mirror Syndication International 6-7
Larry Mulvehill 46-47
The National Archive, Washington , DC 65, 106
  (bottom)
The Newark Museum, Gift of Mrs. Jennie E. Mead,
  1939 75
New England Stock Photo
Kathleen Salerni 90
Michael Shedlock 56
Kevin Shields 58-59
New York Public Library 19
The Picture Cube
Walter Bibikow 48-49, 52-53, 110 (left)
Kindra Clineff 114-115, 122-123
Grace Davies 41
Tom Doran 44
Walter Frost, Jr. 120
Jeff Greenberg 52 (top)
Rob Helfrick 166 (right)
D&I McDonald 79
Cindy McIntyre 61

Picture Perfect
Jean S. Buldain 9
Allan Montaine 126
Dale Schicket 68
H. Armstrong Roberts
H.Abernathy 71, 111
T. Algire 67
Camerique 107
R. Kord 21
James P. Rowan 26, 76
Scala/Art Resource, New York 12
Rick Schafer 45
The Shelburne Museum 20
Tom Stack & Associates
Scott Blackman 125
Terry Donnelly 38, 42-43, 98-99, 121
Stock Montage 10
James Strickland 80
Tom Till 112, 118-119, 127
Mark Turner 31 (bottom)
Brian Vanden Brink 55
Jonathan Wallen 52 (bottom), 124

Contents

•

An Elemental Eloquence

*O*ver the past century, dramatic advances in technology have swept through virtually every field, bringing especially drastic changes to transportation, communication, and navigation. Some of today's light stations would be almost unrecognizable to lighthouse engineers of previous eras. Yet the essential role of the lighthouse as guardian of the shores and protector of seafaring vessels remains fixed in our imaginations. And beyond their practical functions, lighthouses stand as architectural monuments, solid and long-lasting evidence of cultural progressions through the millennia. When viewed in relation to its ancient traditions, the lighthouse has known sophisticated automatic equipment for only moments in its illustrious history. The height of its development occurred in much earlier times, when technical developments came much more slowly.

Lighthouses may be highly specialized structures, but their stories seem to have almost universal appeal. All over the country—and indeed, all over the world—people are fascinated by lighthouses. Some are drawn to the diverse architectural styles; though the quintessential model may be a tall tower with a light on top, quite a wide array of design types have been employed in different regions and different eras. Others like the mechanics: how the various lenses were developed, what sources of light were used, and how the fog signal worked. Still others enjoy the human interest aspects of how the keepers and their families lived day to day, how they coped with extreme conditions, and how they risked their lives to rescue mariners in distress. In addressing all these issues, this book also aims to capture some of that inherent romance. In today's high-speed world, the traditional lighthouse is something of an anomaly; it is perhaps the poetry of the lighthouse that keeps the subject alive. The study of lighthouses offers one

the opportunity to dream, to imagine what life was like in other times, to picture one's existence transformed into a life of gentle solitude with only the sea as a constant companion.

In his eloquent introduction to *Lighthouses of the Maine Coast and the Men Who Keep Them* (written in 1935 by Robert Thayer Sterling, assistant keeper of Portland Head Light), Robert P. Tristram Coffin explores this power of the lighthouse to sway the imagination: "Our lighthouses are . . . survivals of ancient temples dedicated to the ancient religion of light . . . houses that mean both service and beauty. They are the ancestors of the beacons which go across the continents now and guide the new ships of the air on their night ways. They mean more than ornament and service, too. For they are connected with elemental eloquences, fire and wind and ancient worshipping." After thousands of years of faithful service, the lighthouse transcends its obsolescence and remains a cultural icon, a glowing salutation shining out from the darkness.

CHAPTER ONE

Illuminating the Past

The world's first lighthouse was the Pharos of Alexandria (seen here in a 1901 visualization), built in the late third century B.C. The immense tower lit the harbor for more than a thousand years. *Alexandria, Egypt*

Travel has always been an inherent part of human civilization. For thousands of years, people have journeyed to find new sources of food, to establish new settlements, or to explore new lands. From earliest times, voyages by sea posed a particular kind of danger, since primitive navigation methods proved little help in negotiating unknown coastlines or even pinpointing a ship's location in known territory. Natural markers such as familiar rock formations, groupings of tall trees, or mountains served as rudimentary navigational aids. The very first lighthouses were undoubtedly volcanoes, since their fiery effusions were visible both day and night, even far out at sea. Early mariners also learned to rely on bonfires lit along the shore. Once people discovered that elevated fires could be seen at greater distances than those on the beach, they started building tall stone towers to burn fires on top. And with this innovation began the legacy of one of the most important and fascinating structures in history.

This first-century lighthouse, now in ruins, helped Roman ships navigate around the tiny island of Capri, just south of Naples. *Capri, Italy*

Does not this unhappy accident evince the necessity of

having a Lighthouse at the entrance of our harbor?

It is supposed that the loss of this vessel was occasioned

by the want of one.

—Cumberland Gazette, *Portland, Maine, February 1787*

LIGHTHOUSES OF THE ANCIENT WORLD

When the ancient world catalogued its Seven Wonders, one of the entries on this remarkable list was a lighthouse. The Pharos of Alexandria, built during the late third century B.C., is considered the world's first lighthouse. Towering above the western entrance of Egypt's Alexandria Harbor on the island of Pharos, the structure stood about 450 feet tall (137.25 m) and rested on a 100-foot (30.5 m) square base that held 300 rooms for the workmen and keepers. Atop this immense base sat three stories, the first two containing steep winding stairs and the third holding the tower's mighty lantern. At the very top stood a statue of Poseidon, god of the seas. Probably made of white

OPPOSITE
Although a seventeenth-century artist has placed a flaming torch in the hand of the Colossus of Rhodes and filled the harbor with ships, evidence suggests that the statue most likely did not actually serve as a lighthouse.

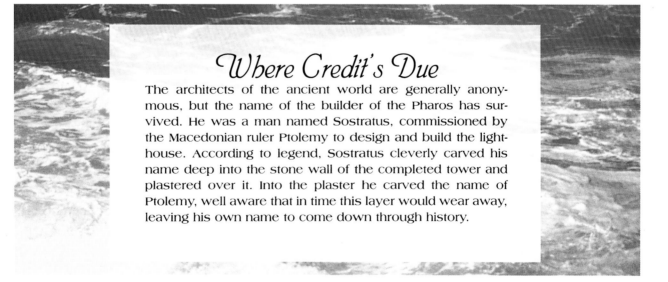

Where Credit's Due

The architects of the ancient world are generally anonymous, but the name of the builder of the Pharos has survived. He was a man named Sostratus, commissioned by the Macedonian ruler Ptolemy to design and build the lighthouse. According to legend, Sostratus cleverly carved his name deep into the stone wall of the completed tower and plastered over it. Into the plaster he carved the name of Ptolemy, well aware that in time this layer would wear away, leaving his own name to come down through history.

limestone, the tower was adorned with elaborate marble carvings and may have stood in the center of a vast courtyard surrounded by lush gardens.

The light of the Pharos was most likely produced by fires tended ceaselessly by slaves, who also performed the arduous task of carting the wood to the tower's summit The lantern may also have held giant reflectors to increase the light's visibility, which reached a distance of 42 miles (67.57 km). At times, particularly during the day, the voluminous smoke that expelled forth from the Pharos served as an even better guide than the fire.

The Pharos lit the skies for more than ten centuries, impressing the likes of Julius Caesar and Pliny the Elder, and the mighty tower endured unlighted for another five hundred years. Its service endured many serious disruptions, including the seventh-century destruction of its lantern during the Arab conquest of Egypt. Several earthquakes wrought damage over the years, and finally an earthquake in the fourteenth century brought the structure to ruins. Yet even in its final years it had remained awe-inspiring; not long before its destruction a visitor declared that "the whole is imperishable, although the waves of the sea continually break against its northern face."

Renowned for their skill and pride in building roads, bridges, walls, aqueducts, and many other structures, the Romans left strangely few records of their lighthouses. Tradition holds that they erected at least thirty lighthouses, the best known and largest of which was a four-story tower built about 50 A.D.; it stood at Ostia, the port of Rome, at the mouth of the River Tiber. Ravenna, on the Adriatic Sea in northern Italy, also received a lighthouse, probably as early as the first century; by the fourth century this city had become a major center of

OPPOSITE
To facilitate expanding trade activity, maritime countries throughout Europe began to increase the number of lighthouses along their coasts. An eighteenth-century painting by Cioci Antonio depicts the lighthouse and port at Villa La Tana, Italy.

Lighthouse designs the world over share common general plans. This cross-sectional view shows the plan of a German lighthouse.

trade and certainly a logical place for a lighthouse, with a harbor capable of accommodating well over two hundred ships. Another of the Seven Wonders, the Colossus of Rhodes, was said to have served as an aid to navigators, with lights maintained in the statue's eyes or raised hand, but there is little evidence that the immense figure ever really served as a lighthouse.

The Romans also placed lighthouses in their provinces, including one on each side of the English Channel. The towers they built on the cliffs of Boulogne in France and the cliffs of Dover in England were most likely the first ones installed in Western Europe after its conquest by Rome. Choosing these elevated sites made the towers less costly; with only 80 feet (24.4 m) of construction they achieved lights that soared almost 400 feet (122 m) above the sea.

MEDIEVAL LIGHTHOUSES

Early lights were generally built close to shore in more accessible areas, to which supplies could be brought easily. But rocks and reefs many miles offshore also presented great danger to ships. One of the earliest and most courageous offshore efforts to erect a lighthouse occurred 5 miles (8.04 km) off the coast of France on the small island of Cordouan. According to legend, the first navigational aid on the island came at the behest of Charlemagne himself, who had a chapel built on the island and ordered the sounding of trumpets to warn passing vessels. Erected in the ninth century as an aid to ships in the Bordeaux wine trade, the first lighthouse on the site was supposedly built by Charlemagne's son

OPPOSITE
The rays of the setting sun peek through the lens of the inactive Cape Meares Lighthouse, making it appear to be lit. *Tillamook, Oregon*

A Light by Any Other Name

The only one of the Seven Wonders with daily practical application, the Pharos served for so long and became so famous that some version of this word means lighthouse in many different languages. Pharus, the Latin term, gave rise to the French phare and the Italian faro. The study of lighthouses is known in English as pharology, another word that owes its derivation to this ancient structure.

The Skerryvore Lighthouse, off the coast of Scottland, was built to withstand the punishing currents of the North Sea.

SKERRYVORE LIGHTHOUSE, ON THE COAST OF SCOTLAND.

Louis the Pious. Supported by funds collected from the area's ships, the Cordouan light was tended by monks, a common practice throughout the medieval period.

A new lighthouse erected on Cordouan in the late fourteenth century included a chapel and living quarters for the monks. By the late sixteenth century this lighthouse had become irreparable and an elaborate replacement was constructed. Intended to take two years, this extremely difficult undertaking wound up taking more than twenty. Simply ferrying the workers to and from this distant site required six boats. Once building began it was discovered that the island was beginning to disappear, so a sturdy wall and parapet were constructed in an attempt to stave off the encroaching sea. Eventually a magnificent structure resulted, complete with statues, pillars, a royal chapel, and a room for the king. In an unusual variation, the spiral staircase was located off to the side to prevent the main portion of the structure from becoming soiled by workers bringing wood and equipment up to the lantern. The ornate tower attained the height of a sixteen-story building, only to lose 25 feet (7.62 m) off the top when it was struck by lightning in 1612. Yet it continued to serve for hundreds of years and helped to convince naysayers that it was indeed possible to construct a workable lighthouse in the middle of the sea.

As trading activity increased during the Middle Ages, England, Ireland, France, Germany, Turkey, and Italy recognized the need for more lighthouses to illuminate their coasts and facilitate their additional shipping capabilities. One of the most famous Italian lighthouses is the one at Genoa, where Antonio Colombo, uncle of Christopher Columbus, served as keeper in 1449. First built in the twelfth century, the original lighthouse was

The Importance of Cordouan

Although most of Cordouan's elaborate ornamentation was lost due to lightning in 1612 and to renovations in the late 1700s, the tower still stands today, the oldest extant wave-swept lighthouse in the world. It is also the world's tallest rock light, and was the site that Augustin Fresnel chose in 1822 to test his revolutionary new lens.

replaced in 1544 by two square brick towers, one on top of the other. Reaching a height of 200 feet (61 m), the structure was susceptible to lightning damage and a lightning rod was finally installed in 1778, after several centuries of unsuccessful belief that a nearby statue of St. Christopher would fend off storm damage. This lighthouse, now used as a daymark for the port of Genoa, is deemed the tallest lighthouse still in operation.

THE MOST FAMOUS LIGHT OF ALL

Off the southwest coast of England lies one of the world's most dangerous underwater reefs. For hundreds of years this cruel array of rock—known as the Eddystone Reef—made for extremely hazardous maritime traffic out of Plymouth, one of the country's most important ports. The word eddystone actually means "stone of reeling waters," and indeed the captain of the *Mayflower*, which sailed from Plymouth in 1620, declared it to be a formation of "great ragged stones around which the sea constantly eddies, a grave danger to all ships hereabouts . . . and always to be dreaded by mariners." Coupled with the perils of the site's jagged rocks, the colliding currents of the Atlantic and the English Channel spelled doom for countless ships.

These lethal rocks presented small opportunity for supporting a much-needed lighthouse. Luckily, a mechanical genius named Harry Winstanley was to provide a solution. After two of his own trading ships were lost upon the Eddystone rocks, he journeyed to Plymouth himself and in 1696 began constructing the first of four lighthouses that would mark the Eddystone Reefs. Hampered by the site's merciless conditions, construction lasted for three years, and Winstanley's unusual polygonal tower lit the seas for five years until the worst storm

OPPOSITE
The wild seas and jagged rocks seen in Thomas Cole's *View across Frenchman's Bay* from Mount Desert Island after a Squall, 1845 clearly illustrate why a longtime commissioner of the Bureau of Lighthouses considered the station at Mount Desert Rock to be the most exposed in the whole United States.

The second of Eddystone Light's four incarnations began operation in 1699. After builder Harry Winstanley deemed his original tower inadequate, he used it as a core and built this structure around and above it. While attempting repairs during a severe storm in November 1703, Winstanley and his crew disappeared—along with the lighthouse itself. *Plymouth, England*

in England's history reduced it to a few broken iron rods protruding from the rocks.

No one doubted that an immediate replacement was needed. The second builder, a silk merchant named John Rudyerd, reasoned that a tower built of timber—because of wood's more flexible nature—would better withstand the fearsome seas than stone. Seeking design help from shipbuilders, he constructed a conical tower of oak and granite, carefully fitting the timbers together and waterproofing them with pitch, like a ship. Rudyerd's tower endured for fifty-two years. But wood, of course, poses one key danger, realized when the lantern caught fire in 1755 and burned the structure to the ground.

Engineer John Smeaton, who built the third lighthouse, dovetailed granite blocks together so carefully that his tower actually outlived the rock on which it sat. After 125 years of service, the upper portion of the lighthouse was moved to Plymouth when its rock base began to erode. The lower portion, known as Smeaton's Stump, is still visible on its original site. Finally, in 1882, the fourth lighthouse was erected on a nearby rock. Originally lit by circular oil wicks, the tower was electrified in 1959 and continues to operate today. Immortalized in a folk song and generally considered the granddaddy of all modern lighthouses, the Eddystone Light was a true successor to the steadfast Pharos of Alexandria and served as a model for many other lighthouses, including a number of towers in America.

Sources of Light

Fueled by wood fires, the lights of early towers were generally exposed to the elements. Covered lanterns later provided some protection from the rain, and after that some structures add glass to further safeguard the flame. But constant burning devoured wood quite swiftly, so by the sixteenth century coal use became more common. Although coal fires presented an increased hazard (a strong wind could create a flame so hot it might melt the grate that contained it), coal fires offered better light and were therefore used for centuries, until the mid-1800s.

OPPOSITE
Dangerous, rocky shores require reliable lights for the most practical of reasons, but the nature of these rugged settings make lighthouses picturesque photography subjects. *Florence, Oregon*

The fog comes
on little cat feet.
It sits looking
over the harbor and city
on silent haunches
And then moves on.

—Carl Sandburg

English Lighthouse Administration

The lighthouses of England have for hundreds of years been overseen by Trinity House, a corporation that arose from the mariners' guild of the Middle Ages. Even though the guilds functioned as independent organizations, they eventually achieved a unity. The Trinity House as Newcastle was the first one empowered to build and maintain lighthouses; to do so it was authorized to collect duties from ships to pay for the projects. Most countries preferred to fund their lighthouses out of the general treasury as a service to the nation; England was one of the few to charge users for their navigational aids. When the Trinity House of Deptford Strond assumed responsibility for all English lighthouses in 1836, it immediately instituted improvements in the condition of that country's lights and the treatment of its keepers.

Now inactive, Price Creek Lighthouse was
erected to guide vessels through the mouth of
the Cape Fear River, part of a dangerous
expanse of waters along the southern coast of
North Carolina. *Southport, North Carolina*

CHAPTER TWO
Building the Towers

*M*ore than a thousand years ago, Viking sea charts labeled the Cape Cod region *Straumey*, meaning "an island possessed of strong currents." But most early European voyagers lacked even primitive maps of these new lands, and for centuries the uncharted shores of North America presented unknown hazards to sailors brave enough to explore the coast. With no lights visible to brighten night skies at sea, the only navigational aids available were crude shipboard tools, seafaring experience, and maritime instinct. As more and more ships reached the New World, inhabitants began lighting signal fires along the coast to guide their way. In 1673, on the bleak headland of Point Allerton near Boston, was lit the first primitive approximation of a lighthouse in the Americas. Though hardly more than a light on a pole, it was a beginning.

EARLY LIGHTS IN THE NEW WORLD

The history of American lighthouses officially begins in 1716. At the request of the area's merchants, the Province of Massachusetts that

The harbour lies below me, with, on the far side, one long granite wall stretching out into the sea, with a curve outwards at the end of it, in the middle of which is a lighthouse.

—*Bram Stoker,* Dracula

Ye Gentlemen of England
    That live at home at ease
Ah! little do you think upon
        The Dangers of the seas.

—Martin Parker

year erected a "Light Hous and Lanthorn on some Head Land at the Entrance of the Harbor of Boston for the Direction of Ships and Vessels in the Night Time bound into the said Harbor." This harbor also became the site of the country's first fog signal when a cannon was installed in 1719. Over the next seven decades the Colonies erected twelve more lights, ranging from Brant Point Light in Massachusetts to Tybee Island Light in Georgia.

At the end of the American Revolution, foreign trade was an immediate problem facing the fledging country and its new states. Each state at first retained control over its lighthouses, but when the federal government organized in 1789, it immediately assumed responsibility for the operation of all navigational aids. The new administration soon undertook the building of several lighthouses, including one at Portland off Maine's southern coast, where construction had been spurred by a nearby sloop wreck in

Lighthouse Tragedy

George Worthylake, Boston Light's first keeper, had served for two years when disaster struck. Returning to the lighthouse one day, he and his family drowned when their boat capsized during a storm. Benjamin Franklin, then thirteen years old, heard of the drowning and wrote a ballad called "Lighthouse Tragedy" to memorialize the incident. His brother printed sheet music of the song, which young Franklin sold on the streets of Boston. Citizens were saddened to learn of the great tragedy that had befallen their lighthouse.

When Florida joined the United States in 1821, St. Augustine was the principal port. The small harbor light installed in 1824 proved insufficient, and the Lighthouse Board determined that a seacoast light was needed. After many construction difficulties, St. Augustine Lighthouse began service in 1874. *Anastasia Island, Florida*

1787. A partial tower already existed on the site when the federal government assumed control in 1790; Congress then appropriated funds to finish the project. In 1791, Portland Head Light began operation as the first lighthouse completed by the new government. The next light to see service was in 1792 at Chesapeake Bay's Cape Henry. Constructed entirely with federal funds, it became the country's first public works project.

As the center of the early United States shipping industry, New England was the hub of United States lighthouse construction. In addition, since lighthouses were generally built in response to local appeals for navigational aids, louder entreaties were more likely to come from the more heavily populated Northeast. The concentration of shipping activities in the New England region continued after the Revolution, and by the mid-1820s almost two-thirds of the country's lights stood between Maine's West Quoddy Head (built in 1858) and New York's Montauk Point (1797) and Fire Island Light (1826). About half the lights built in the first decade

The original first-order lens of Cape Blanco Lighthouse, installed in 1870 and still in operation, is rated at one million candlepower. *Port Orford, Oregon*

OPPOSITE
Cape Lookout Lighthouse, built in 1859, has a unique diamond daymark pattern. Daymarks are used to make lighthouses more visible when the sun is shining; in northern climates, they also help make these landmarks stand out in the snow. *Beaufort, North Carolina*

Eldred Rock Lighthouse, one of the state's oldest surviving lights, was constructed in 1906 to guide vessels along the Lynn Canal. *Haines, Alaska*

Lighthouse Administration

As its ninth official act, the first Congress in 1789 placed the operation of all navigational aids under the central government's jurisdiction: "In the necessary support, maintenance and repairs of all lighthouses, beacons, buoys and public piers erected, placed, or sunk before the passing of this act, at the entrance of, or within any bay, inlet, harbor, or port of the United States, for rendering the navigation thereof easy and safe, shall be defrayed out of the Treasury of the United States." The Bureau of Lighthouses was established on August 7, 1789, under the auspices of the Treasury Department and the direction of the Secretary of the Treasury.

As a result of the Lighthouse Bureau's detailed investigations to increase individual light station efficiency, the Lighthouse Board was formed October 9, 1852. The board remained part of the Treasury Department until July 1, 1903, when the Department of Commerce and Labor took control of it. On July 1, 1939, President Roosevelt transferred duties to the United States Coast Guard, under whose jurisdiction lighthouse administration remains today.

Until 1852, lighthouse construction had been awarded by contract, with few regulations for guidance other than a simple sketch and brief specifications. The Lighthouse Board began setting much stricter standards; its drawings and preparatory information were so extensive that little innovation was left to the builders. Since assuming control of lighthouse administration in 1939, the Coast Guard has employed its own designers.

To see! To see! This is the craving of the sailor . . . I have heard a reserved silent man, with no nerves to speak of, after three days of hard running in thick water, burst out passionately, "I wish to God we could get sight of something!"

—Joseph Conrad

The Long and Short of It

With its low coasts, the southeastern United States requires very high towers. Rising to 193 feet (58.86 m), Cape Hatteras is the tallest brick lighthouse in the country. On the West Coast, where cliffs soar high above the Pacific, the towers themselves often require minimal height because of their lofty perches. At 43 feet (13.11 m) tall, northern California's Cape Mendocino Lighthouse is one of the shortest in the nation, but its location places the light at 465 feet (141.82 m) above the ocean. Reaching 348 feet (106.14 m), the tallest lighthouse in the world is located in Yokohama, Japan.

of the nineteenth century marked harbor or bay entrances, such as those at Cape Cod's Chatham Harbor (1808) and Whitehead Island (1807) in Maine's Penobscot Bay. Rhode Island's Point Judith Light (1809) helped ships into Narragansett Bay. Connecticut received a light at Black Rock Harbor (1809). Portsmouth, New Hampshire, a key shipbuilding port during the Revolution, had seen the construction of a colonial lighthouse in 1771, which required rebuilding in 1804.

By the 1810s, even though most new construction still centered in the North, more lighthouses began to be built south of Delaware Bay. The dangerous stretch of coast around the Carolinas eventually earned the unhappy appellation of "Graveyard of the Atlantic." The first tower at North Carolina's Cape Hatteras went up in 1803; by the mid-nineteenth century it was considered the most important East Coast light and a new tower was erected to improve visibility. Until 1848, when Bodie Island obtained a light, no tower lit the perilous eighty-mile stretch from that site north to Virginia's Cape Henry. Many more lighthouses arose along the Eastern seaboard throughout the century, ranging as far south as Florida's Jupiter Inlet (1860).

As the shipping industry spread through the Great Lakes—which present many of the same navigational hazards as the ocean—the pressing need for lighthouses was quickly recognized. The region's very first light was built by Canada in 1804; the first two United States lights, erected in 1819, were Lake Erie's Presque Isle Light and Buffalo Light. Dozens more were erected on all the Great Lakes over the next century.

OPPOSITE
The Italianate style of the Point Fermin Lighthouse saw many changes over the years, but the structure has now been restored to its original 1874 appearance. *San Pedro, California*

This 1872 woodcut shows the deserted Bar Light House at the mouth of Florida's St. John's River.

Similar in design to other important lights on the eastern shore of Lake Michigan, Grand Haven South Pierhead Inner Light stands in bright contrast to the colors of winter. *Ottawa County, Michigan*

OPPOSITE
Lights mounted on pilings were uised as simple beacons to aid navigators, but were also used by wreckers to lure shops into dangerous waters

PREVIOUS PAGE
The distinctive daymark pattern of West Quoddy Head Lighthouse has made it one of the country's best-known lighthouses. Situated at the easternmost point of the continental United States, this famous light helps steer vessels through the Bay of Fundy. *Lubec, Maine*

When the western territories joined the United States in 1846, the government discovered that the entire expanse of coast from northern Washington to southern California contained not a single navigational aid. The first Pacific Coast lighthouse was established on San Francisco Bay in 1852, on Alcatraz Island. The original tower was torn down in 1909 to make room for the infamous maximum-security prison and a new one constructed nearby. Fifteen more West Coast lights followed in rapid succession over the next six years.

LIGHTHOUSE CONSTRUCTION

To many people the quintessential lighthouse is a tall stone tower. For centuries this style was the general rule, and many brick or stone lighthouses were modeled on the Eddystone Light. Yet lighthouses actually take numerous forms,

Record Holders

The oldest tower in America still in operation is the octagonal Sandy Hook Light in New Jersey. Built by New York merchants in 1764, it survived repeated attacks during the Revolution and is the only colonial lighthouse still standing.

The United States lighthouse located farthest from shore is Stannard Rock Lighthouse. Standing some 23 miles (37 km) north of Michigan on Lake Superior, the tower was erected in 1882 on a shoal the Lighthouse Board had called "the most serious danger to navigation in Lake Superior."

Behold, now, another providence of God.
A ship comes into the harbor.

—William Bradford

The lighthouse and Coast Guard Station of Muskegon (seen in a watercolor by Robert Wilson Fagan) help vessels along the eastern shore of Lake Michigan.

OPPOSITE
Originally stationed on Chesapeake Bay to guide ships into Baltimore Harbor, Seven-Foot Knoll Lighthouse was later moved to a museum setting. It is the oldest surviving screwpile light from the bay. *Baltimore, Maryland*

with the type of construction dependent on the importance of the light and the conditions of the foundation. Harbor or lake lights often combined a tower and a dwelling of timber or brick, though in the more important lights the tower was generally detached from the dwelling. Most older towers of this type were built of brick or stone masonry, with cast iron stairways and lanterns. Indicative of the East Coast origins of Pacific lighthouse, the Cape Cod style was first used on the West Coast in the 1850s. The design consisted of a squarish dwelling with a tower rising directly from the roof.

The sturdy masonry complex of Admiralty Head Lighthouse, built in 1903, contained a fourth-order Fresnel lens that served until 1927. After years of disuse, the structure is now refurbished and is open to the public. *Coupeville, Washington*

I remember the wharves and the slips
And the sea-tides tossing free
And Spanish sailors with bearded lips,
And the beauty and mystery of ships
And the magic of the sea.

—Henry Wadsworth Longfellow

Other situations called for design innovations. To combat foundations consisting of shifting sand or to provide a base far out in the water, the pile lighthouse employed long iron legs sunk deep into the foundation. In 1850, Minots Ledge—south of Boston—became the first such light in the United States to use this construction. A variation of this type was the screw-pile light, employed frequently around Chesapeake Bay and the Gulf Coast. It utilized broad screw flanges attached to iron rods bored like an auger into the bottom of the site. The legs were then braced to make the seating even more secure, and the lighthouse built on a platform set on top of this configuration. For sites on a muddy sea floor, the caisson light was widely used in the United States, beginning at Duxbury, Massachusetts, in 1871. A cast-iron cylinder was sunk into the ocean floor and filled with concrete to form a secure base. Many lights at harbor entrances were built on ends of breakwaters or pierheads, with construction similar to that used on shore. Pierhead and breakwater lighthouses, generally made of metal in varying styles, are common throughout the Great Lakes region.

Besides the tower itself, light stations often featured a number of other buildings, such as an oil house, workshops, a boat house, outbuildings, and of course, keeper's quarters. The dwelling might consist of one, two, or three stories, sometimes connected to the tower by a covered passageway. Of all buildings on the site, it was the keeper's residence that most clearly displayed the prevailing architecture of the region and the era.

With the only red lens on the West Coast, the beam from the Umpqua River Lighthouse can be seen from over twenty miles. *Winchester Bay, Oregon.*

OPPOSITE
Only 26 feet tall, Owls Head Lighthouse is nestled on a promontory that raises the focal plane to 100 feet, making the light visible for 16 miles at sea. *Rockland, Maine*

Fresnel Classifications

Classed according to size as measured by the focal distance of the lens (from the center of the light to the inner surface of the lens), Fresnel lenses range from first order down to sixth order. First-order lens measure 36.2 inches (91.9 cm); second, 27.6 inches (70.1 cm); third, 19.7 inches (50 cm); third-and-a-half, 14.7 inches (37.3 cm); fourth, 9.8 inches (24.9 cm); fifth, 7.4 inches (18.8 cm); and sixth, 5.9 inches (14.9 cm).

On April 3, 1884, the steamer *Daniel Steinmann* was wrecked near Nova Scotia's Sambro Lighthouse. This newspaper illustration depicts the scene of the wreck.

OPPOSITE
First built in 1825 and given additional elevation in 1885, Cape Florida Lighthouse is the oldest light in the state and the oldest standing structure of any kind in south Florida. *Key Biscayne, Florida*

Before the first Bodie Island Lighthouse was built in 1848, the eighty-mile shore from Cape Hatteras to Cape Henry was a perilous, unlit stretch. The third light to stand on the sight, the present black-and-white tower was lighted in 1872. *Dare County, North Carolina*

LIGHTING THE LIGHTS

The most crucial element of the lighthouse—the light itself—evolved slowly as technology improved. At first, open coal or wood fires burned on a brazier atop the tower. The first Boston Light is believed to have been lit with tallow candles. Colonial lighthouses often used wick lamps that burned whale oil or fish oil. When that became scarce, they might resort to a form of vegetable oil called colza or to lard from animal fat. As the lamp wick burned it had to be trimmed fre-

From Clee to heaven the beacon burns,
The shires have seen it plain,
From north and south the sign returns
And beacons burn again.

—A.E. Houseman

Though the skeletal ironwork of Rawley Point Lighthouse looks surprisingly modern, it was erected in 1894 to replace a brick tower built twenty years earlier, contemporaneous with the dwelling. *Two Rivers, Wisconsin*

OPPOSITE
Renowned for its twin light towers, the community of Cape Elizabeth was outraged in 1924 when the Bureau of Lighthouses declared an end to multiple-tower stations. Though only the eastern tower still stands, the station is still commonly known as Two Lights. Edward Hopper's The Lighthouse at Two Lights was painted five years after the western tower was dismantled. *Cape Elizabeth, Maine*

PREVIOUS PAGE
Most lighthouses are equipped with a number of other buildings, such as a boathouse and keeper's quarters. The clean design of the 1876 cylindrical iron, brick-lined tower of Nobska Point Lighthouse compliments the stark lines of the buildings beside it. *Falmouth, Massachusetts*

quently to keep the lamp from smoking. The late 1700s saw the introduction of oil-burning spider lamps, which were suspended by iron chains from the top of the lantern. Though they emitted better light, keepers found their caustic fumes intolerable.

A major innovation occurred in 1781 when Swiss physicist Aimé Argand developed a lamp that utilized a hollow wick, allowing more air to flow around the flame. The additional oxygen made for a much brighter flame. Around 1812, the power of the Argand lamp was increased with the addition of parabolic reflectors and a magnifier.

The World's Largest Lens

The Stevensons were an extraordinary family of Scottish lighthouse engineers who dominated their country's lighthouse service throughout the nineteenth century and well into this one. (Novelist Robert Louis Stevenson, who began his career as a lighthouse engineer, was a fourth-generation member of the Stevenson lighthouse clan.) They developed a type of lens called the hyperradiant lens, whose focal distance—measured from the light to the inside of the lens—makes it the largest lens ever produced. The hyperradiant lens has a focal distance of over 52 inches (132 cm), compared to 36 inches (91.4 cm) for a first-order Fresnel. Only about twelve lenses of this type were in use throughout the world in the early twentieth century.

The only hyperradiant lens ever acquired by the United States was installed in 1909 at Makapuu Lighthouse. Located on the island of Oahu, this site was deemed in need of a lighthouse in 1905, when the Lighthouse Board declared, "All deep-sea commerce between Honolulu and Puget Sound, the Pacific coast of the United States, Mexico and Central America, including Panama, passes Makapuu Head, and . . . there is not a single light on the whole northern coast of the Hawaiian Islands to guide ships or warn them of their approach to land, after a voyage of several thousand miles." Now automated, the still-active light at Makapuu boasts an immense lens with an inside diameter of 8.5 feet (2.59 m).

Aye on the shores of darkness there is light,

And precipices show untrodden green,

There is a budding morrow in midnight,

There is a triple sight in blindness keen.

—John Keats

Built in 1827, Pemaquid
Point Lighthouse received
its fourth-order Fresnel
lens in the 1850s. The
light was automated in
1934. *Pemaquid Point,
Maine*

OPPOSITE
Stone structures have proven
to be the most durable
kind of lighthouse. After a gale
destroyed the first, wooden
lighthouse in 1816, a stone
replacement was built at the
entrance to Narragansett
Bay. The current granite tower
of Point Judith Lighthouse
was erected in 1856.
Narragansett, Rhode Island

Deemed by the Lighthouse
Board a "very important light,"
Montauk Lighthouse was
ranked tenth of the nation's
thirty-eight light stations
that required first-order lens.
Long Island, New York

The true breakthrough in lighthouse illumination came about 1815 when an engineer named Augustin-Jean Fresnel invented the most efficient lighthouse lens of all. Resembling a beehive, the Fresnel lens consisted of a configuration of glass belts to magnify and refract light. By 1859, Fresnel lenses had replaced reflectors in most United States lighthouses. Sperm oil was still the most common illuminant, but because it was costly, lard oil became standard in the 1860s and was widely used until 1877, when kerosene gained prominence. Although electricity was introduced in the early twentieth century, it did not become universally employed for several decades. Many of today's electric lighthouses still employ the Fresnel lens.

CHAPTER THREE
Lonely at the Top

ver the past hundred years, advances in technology permitted steady improvements in lighthouse functions, to the point where most are now fully automated and require only occasional human intervention. But for more than two thousand years, constant human involvement was essential to lighthouse operation. Nowadays the concept of tending a lighthouse has a romantic aura about it, symbolizing escape from the stresses of urban life to a tranquil seaside setting. But the countless men and women—and even children—who undertook keeper's duties also undertook a life of solitude and monotony, and of utter dedication to their work.

THE LIFE OF THE KEEPER

In today's world of automated lighthouses, swift transportation, and electronic communications, it is difficult to realize the extremes of isola-

Anythin' for a quiet life, as the man said
wen he took the sitivation at the lighthouse.

—*Charles Dickens,* Pickwick Papers

tion and hardship that for centuries comprised the day-to-day existence of the lighthouse keeper. Set in secluded locations, light stations offered no community in which to raise a family, no markets at which to obtain provisions, no schools for the children, and no neighbors with whom to socialize. Even passing ships avoided the area if the keeper performed the job well. Yet the occupation was not without its rewards, and most keepers took great pride in their work, finding satisfaction in the knowledge that they provided their country with an invaluable service.

The most important task at any lighthouse was of course to keep the light itself in good working order. Until the nineteenth century, this often entailed refilling the oil in as many as thirty lamps several times a night, keeping the wicks lit, and cleaning the smoke buildup off the lantern's windows. The introduction of the Argand lamp certainly improved the situation, but it brought with it the new task of cleaning the reflectors

Decoding the Signal

All lighthouse lights are white, red, green, or a combination thereof. A ship captain times the flashes and refers to a light list to determine which lighthouse is sending the signals and thus to pinpoint the ship's position. Before the introduction of machinery, lights were usually fixed. Once an apparatus became available to enable the lens to revolve, light and dark periods could be made to produce variations, referred to as the light's characteristic. The basic types are fixed, flashing (a single flash at regular intervals), fixed and flashing (a fixed light varied at regular intervals by a single, greater flash), group flashing (groups of flashes at regular intervals), and occulting (a steady light suddenly and completely eclipsed by two or more periods of total darkness at regular intervals). These characteristics all refer to lights of one color (generally white); lights that change color are known as "alternating." "Flashing" means the length of the flash is shorter than the time of darkness; "occulting" indicates that the dark period is shorter than or equal to the duration of light.

OPPOSITE
Spiral staircases are common inside lighthouse towers, where solitary keepers made frequent trips up and down the winding steps. The masonry tower of Michigan Island Lighthouse—the oldest of the Apostle lights— houses an iron staircase that spirals up to a black lantern. *Apostle Islands, Wisconsin*

Off-shore lighthouse keepers received few visitors—even delivering provisions proved to be a dangerous trip.

OPPOSITE
Connected to land by a thin wooden bridge, Marshall Point Lighthouse the short trek from the keeper's house to the light could be dangerous in stormy weather. *Port Clyde, Maine*

PREVIOUS PAGE
The job might be lonely, but the keeper's house usually has a fantastic view. Perched on a crag in beautiful Acadia National Park, Bass Harbor Head Lighthouse continues to help steer vessels around the harbor. *Ellsworth, Maine*

that backed each lamp. Once rotating lens were installed to enable lights to flash a particular pattern, keepers had to wind and clean the clockworks by which the lenses operated.

The job required someone with stamina, skill, dexterity, and patience; someone knowledgeable about lighthouse routine and about the handling of boats. Not only did keepers have to contend with an unending round of daily chores, they had to learn to perform them with very little training. Each lighthouse lantern was supposed to display an instruction sheet detailing the workings of the lighting system, but many stations lacked even this single page of directions. A new keeper might receive a crash course from the outgoing keeper, but much of the learning must have occurred on the job itself. When the Lighthouse Board was established in the mid-nineteenth century, it began issuing more thorough written instructions and established the requirement that keepers could not be hired unless they were able to read.

The board's extensive regulations specified that maintenance work be divided into two "departments" at stations with two or more keep-

Now is the stately column broke
The beacon-light is quench'd in smoke,
The strumpet's silver sound is still,
The warder silent on the hill!

—*Sir Walter Scott*

The precarious placement of lighthouse on wave-beaten shores makes them particularly vulnerable to damage and erosion. The St. Marks Lighthouse had to be moved in the 1840s to protect it from erosion, and required reconstruction after being damaged during the Civil War. *St. Marks, Florida*

Though most often photographed in seascapes, lighthouse interiors also make picturesque photography subjects. *Copper Harbor, Michigan*

OPPOSITE
The eclectic Fort Tompkins Lighthouse combined a tower with a mansard-roofed house, all decked out in Victorian gingerbread. *Fort Tompkins, New York*

ers. The person in the first department was responsible for polishing the lens, cleaning and filling the lamp, trimming the wicks, and ensuring that all the lighting equipment was ready by ten in the morning for the evening's lighting. The person in the second department polished the metal fixtures of the apparatus, cleaned the walls and floors of the lantern, and swept the stairs and passageways.

When fog hung in the air and obscured visibility—a particular hazard in New England and along the West Coast—the keepers' obligations extended to running the foghorn. Before the introduction of machinery to operate fog signals automatically, this entailed ringing the fog bell or sounding the siren continuously by hand until the sky cleared—sometimes for hours or even days on end.

LIGHTHOUSE FAMILIES

Entire families were often involved in tending a lighthouse. To take charge when the keeper was away or when emergency befell the station, the wife and children of the keeper usually knew how to operate

The Importance of Daymarks

To make lighthouses more recognizable by day, the Lighthouse Board introduced the concept of painting coastal towers in distinctive colors or patterns. Red stripes on American lighthouses generally signal that the tower stands to the right of an important harbor; blue or black stripes mean it is located on the left side. Many towers are painted white, but to enhance visibility in northern regions where snow may supply unwanted camouflage, a contrasting stripe is often added. To this end, vivid red accents appear on a number of lighthouses in northern Maine and eastern Canada, such as West Quoddy Head on the Maine coast, New Brunswick's Head Harbour Light, Prince Edward Island's Covehead, and Nova Scotia's Peggy's Cove. Combinations of black and white in a wide array of patterning distinguish various towers, particularly in the southeastern United States, including North Carolina's Cape Hatteras, Cape Lookout, and Bodie Island; Virginia Beach's Cape Henry, and Florida's St. Augustine and Cape Canaveral. The striking diamond pattern added to Cape Lookout in 1873 even inspired a local community to name itself Diamond City.

For solitude sometimes is best society

And short retirement urges sweet return.

—*John Milton*

the light and perform other essential tasks. Often the keeper's wife officially served as assistant keeper.

The family of the keeper was called on to assist with as many duties as possible. When the daily chores were complete, it was time to turn to general maintenance tasks such as minor equipment repairs, patching cracks in the tower walls, or replacing damaged panes of glass in the lantern. At least once a year the corroded metal of the lantern required refurbishing. If the tower was whitewashed, as many were, it called for the arduous task of repainting, which entailed sitting in a basket far above the ground and hoisting oneself up and down by means of a pulley system. (Women were exempt from participating in this painting task.) The seemingly endless staircase spiraling up into the tower also needed new paint once a year, conducted in a such a way as to keep the stairs usable at all times to reach the lantern. And there was the constant task of polishing the brass, which was quickly dulled by fog and salt water. In addition to the exertions required to make the tower run smoothly, the entire light station needed continual diligence for everything from common housekeeping to detailed recordkeeping.

Though there was little time for idleness with so many chores to complete, lighthouse dwellers did find themselves with occasional time on their hands. In their isolated setting, with no readymade activities to hand nor a community to participate in, keepers and their families had to develop their own recreation. To break the monotony they often took up hobbies such as boat building, wood carving, basket weaving, rug hooking, tailoring, painting, or music. Others devoted

The first light station in British Columbia was the charmingly designed Fisgard Lighthouse, tended by keepers until 1928. *Victoria, British Columbia*

OPPOSITE
One of the West Coast's first eight lights, the old Point Loma Lighthouse was so high—462 feet above the sea—that low clouds often obscured it. Replaced by a newer station in 1891, the original 1855 Cape Cod–style structure now houses an exhibit detailing the life of a keeper's family. *San Diego, California*

Clean lanterns, lenses, and
windows are imperative in
lighthouses, and maintaining
the mechanism was in
itself a full-time job.
Winchester Bay, Oregon

OPPOSITE
Situated to the west of the
entrance to Muscongus Bay,
Pemaquid Point Lighthouse
sits atop spectacular bluffs
that make the station a
popular tourist destination.
Pemaquid Point, Maine

PREVIOUS PAGE
Encased in steel plates painted eye-popping red, Holland
Harbor South Pierhead
Lighthouse features a twin-
gabled roof indicative of the
heavy Dutch influence in the
region. *Holland, Michigan*

themselves to the study of sea birds, seashells, or local artifacts. Also popular were fishing and hunting, which not only provided a diversion but yielded a ready supply of food as well. A monthly excursion to the mainland to buy food and collect mail also offered a much-needed opportunity to do a bit of socializing and to keep up with developments in the outside world.

Growing up in the unique atmosphere of a light station, many sons and daughters of lighthouse keepers knew little of the outside world. Education presented many problems, and keepers' families arrived at various solutions. The nearest schools were generally too far for a daily commute, nor would the prospect of traveling over a rough sea make it any easier. Although many keepers received addi-tional finances for educating their children, wages were usually too low to afford room and board, even though the school itself might be free. And the children themselves, accustomed as they were to a

The keeper's house was more than a home; it was also the schoolroom, recreation area, and library for the keeper's family. As lighthouses have closed or become automated, the attached dwellings have earned new uses. The 1857 dwelling of Pemaquid Point Lighthouse is now home to the Fisherman's Museum.
Pemaquid Point, Maine

remote life, often found it difficult to adjust to life in mainland schools. Some keepers with school-age children sought to transfer to a station that was closer to a school, or made arrangements for their families to live in town.

In the early 1900s, the state of Maine decided to send teachers out to the lighthouses rather than bring reluctant students into school. The keeper's house or the open room at the base of the tower served as a classroom. Like the keepers themselves, these teachers had to possess a sense of adventure and a good deal of stamina. They taught the same subjects covered in mainland schools, and they, in turn, learned much about a unique way of life from their young charges.

OPPOSITE
The extreme hardship experienced by keepers at the Mount Desert Lighthouse (seen here in an 1847 painting by Thomas Doughty) did not prevent them from attempting to garden. By hauling barrels of dirt from the mainland, keepers and their families created small gardens to brighten their lonely outpost. *Mount Desert Rock, Maine*

The Inspector Calls

Although no supervisor stood by to oversee their every move, keepers never knew when the ominous visit from an inspector might occur. Once every quarter, an inspector would appear at a lighthouse unannounced to ensure it was well maintained and spotlessly clean. Keepers and their families dreaded this arrival, knowing the inspector would examine every detail of their work. The wife of one keeper declared, "You never knew when they were comin'. They'd inspect everything in the house. The house belongs to them. They used to run their fingers along the window sills to see if there was dust. We had one inspector . . . [who brought] a handkerchief and he'd run it over the window by your stove, of all places."

If the inspector found that the equipment, dwelling, tower, storage sheds, privies, and everything else at the station was not strictly up to par, the keeper would be issued a warning to improve the situation before the next inspection. Keepers receiving two failing inspections might be subject to dismissal. Most stations, however, did pass inspection, helped in no small part by the fact that a lighthouse under inspection flew the inspector's flag, signaling other stations to jump into action preparing their own station.

The ship was cheered, the harbor cleared,
Merrily did we drop,
Below the kirk, below the hill,
Below the lighthouse top.

—Samuel Taylor Coleridge

In 1876, the Lighthouse Board created circulating libraries offering a wide choice of reading materials to the keepers' family, who anticipated with great delight the arrival of new books every three months. The board ordered the libraries make the rounds of "isolated light-houses of the higher orders, where there are keepers with families, who will read and appreciate the books the Libraries contain." By 1885, over four hundred libraries were in circulation. Each library contained about forty publications, including novels, biographies, religious subjects, and magazines. Many of the books were acquired through donations from people who wanted to help provide diversions for lonely keepers.

The brick tower and dwelling of Point aux Barques Lighthouse—captured here in watercolor by Robert Wilson Fagan—date from an 1857 rebuilding of the station. The second dwelling was added in 1908. *Port Austin, Michigan*

LADIES OF THE LAMP

The position of lighthouse keeper, though typically considered to belong to men, employed a great number of women as well, who were often the wives of keepers and served as assistant keepers. The fifth auditor of the treasury—responsible for lighthouse administration until the advent of the Lighthouse Board—gave particular preference to women from 1820 to 1852, specifying that a recently widowed wife of a keeper should be tendered the job before anyone else. So many women accepted this offer that by 1852 the United States boasted thirty female keepers. Even after the board began discouraging the hiring of women in 1852, many women managed to obtain the job.

After the death of her husband, Kate Walker was appointed to his job as keeper of Staten Island's Robbins Reef Lighthouse, retiring at the age of seventy-three. For years she ferried her two children to school each day, rowing over a mile each way. During her lengthy tenure (from 1896 to 1919), she saved fifty lives by her own estimate. All this at a station that could only be entered by reaching out from her boat, grabbing a shaky ladder, and climbing up into the kitchen.

OPPOSITE
The keeper's quarters and lighthouse at Wind Point combines a 108-foot Italianate brick tower with a traditional Mid-Western style farmhouse on southwestern shore of Lake Michigan. *Racine, Wisconsin*

Perched precariously outside
the lantern, keepers scrub
the glass clean to maintain
maximum brightness from
the station's light.

OPPOSITE
Built in 1871, Yaquina Bay
Lighthouse had served for
only three years when the
Lighthouse Board declared it
unnecessary, since the
Yaquina Head Lighthouse
stood just a few miles away.
Local residents saved the
landmark from planned de-
struction in 1946; it is now a
museum. *Newport, Oregon*

Matinicus Rock Lighthouse, an extremely isolated station on the rugged midcoast of Maine, was home to Abbie
Burgess, one of the most dedicated women to serve as
lighthouse keeper. The daughter of Matinicus Rock's keeper,
Abbie first demonstrated her dedication as a teenager in the
1850s when her father became stranded on the mainland
and she took charge of the station during an incredible four-
week storm that sent waves crashing over their roof, completely flooding the keeper's quarters and forcing them to
take shelter in the tower. In addition to caring for their
invalid mother and coping with the furious storm, she and
her three younger sisters succeeded in running the light
each and every night. A year later she again performed her duties
heroically in her father's absence; this time the storm lasted three
weeks and the family nearly ran out of food, but the light never failed.
In 1861, she married the son of the station's new keeper; together
they ran Matinicus Rock for fourteen years, later transferring to

Lighthouse Gardens

Many lighthouse families were especially fond of gar-
dening, a pastime that—like hunting or fishing—poten-
tially offered provisions as well as entertainment. At
those stations where soil was plentiful, families grew
thriving vegetable gardens and lush flowering plants.
But such was the determination of many families that
even those assigned to stations set on barren cliffs managed to cultivate gardens. So great was their desire to
see things grow that resourceful keepers hauled soil
from the mainland and filled any available rock crevice
with earth, knowing that at any moment a storm might
obliterate their hard work and they would have to begin
building their garden anew.

The epitome of the quaint New England lighthouse, Stage Harbor Light is captured on a snowy winter's day in this watercolor by James Strickland.

OPPOSITE
The compact tower, dwelling, and outbuildings of Prospect Harbor Point Lighthouse sit close to the shore on the rocky Maine coast. *Prospect Harbor, Maine*

Whitehead Light Station, where Abbie remained assistant keeper until 1889.

One of the most renowned keepers of all time was a woman named Ida Lewis. Born in Newport, Rhode Island in 1842, she performed her first rescue at age 15; her last at age 65. When her father, the first keeper of Newport Harbor's Lime Rock Lighthouse, was paralyzed by a stroke soon after his appointment, she assumed his duties. She saved many people, but her most famous and daring rescue occurred during a blizzard in 1869, when she saved three men whose boat had overturned in the raging storm. After *Harper's Weekly* placed her on their cover that year to acknowledge her bravery, people learned of her earlier heroism. Though she regretted her lost privacy, fame brought with it long-overdue recognition of her years of hard work. The governor of Rhode Island learned that she received neither pay nor title for doing a lighthouse keeper's job and his efforts ensured that she was officially appointed to the post. As her fame spread she received many awards, as well as visits from President Ulysses S. Grant and a number of other important officials. When she died in 1911, the Bureau of Lighthouses changed the station's name to the Ida Lewis Rock Lighthouse, one of the very few lights to be named after a person and the only keeper to be so honored.

The last woman lighthouse keeper in the United States was Fannie Salter, who retired from her position after twenty-two years of service at Maryland's Turkey Point Lighthouse on Chesapeake Bay. After her retirement in 1947, the light was given over to automation.

CHAPTER FOUR

In Harm's Way

Lightships were used as navigational aids in the days before hi-tech equipment were available. Anchored off-shore in seas where building a lighthouse was unfeasible, these mobile beacons are now rare.

$\mathcal{S}$ending forth their glowing signals, light houses have always provided essential navigational support and resulted in the safety of innumerable vessels and of countless lives. To perform such duties properly, light stations have had to endure perilous situations themselves. Threatened by merciless storms, wild seas, raging winds, and eroding foundations, the towers and those who kept them have known their own share of danger, just as surely as have the vessels they were meant to save. And yet one group whose history is linked to that of lighthouses eagerly sought the coming of storms, fog, and darkness, for such foes to all vessels and to those tending the lights were precisely what this malevolent faction required for its evil purposes.

Poor naked wretches, wheresoe'er you are,

That bide the pelting of this pitiless storm,

How shall your houseless heads and unfed sides,

Your looped and window'd raggedness, defend you

From seasons such as these?

—*William Shakespeare*, King Lear

We have fed our sea for a thousand years
And she calls us, still unfed,
Though there's never a wave of all her waves
But marks our English dead.

—Rudyard Kipling

THE RAVAGES OF NATURE

As solitary as their lives often were, many keepers must have longed for an even quieter life when faced with the extremes of weather they continually faced. The exposed location of the lighthouse placed it well in the way of many meteorological excesses. Wild winds and torrential rains churned the seas, producing waves of dizzying heights, often tall enough to sweep over the lantern. Lightning damaged many a tower until lightning rods were eventually installed. Hurricanes have toppled a number of lights, including the first Key West lighthouse, Rhode Island's Prudence Island light, and Palmer Island light in New Bedford, Massachusetts. In 1938, a terrible hurricane ravaged many New England lighthouses. Winter storms were also particularly taxing: Blizzards and ice buildup obscured visibility, interfered with station functions, and sometimes trapped keepers inside or prevented them from entering; and bone-chilling cold made even the simplest tasks arduous.

Minot's Ledge Light is considered by many to be the nation's most dangerous lighthouse. Located near Cohasset, just south of Boston, the treacherously rocky and wave-swept offshore region witnessed many shipwrecks before an iron-pile light was begun in 1847. When the station went into service in 1850, the keeper expressed doubts about the structure's durability. His successor also came to doubt its ability to withstand the extremes of the site's conditions. After a terrible gale in April 1851, the local paper declared, "Great apprehensions are

A Unique Winter Hazard

Coastal lighthouses experience a wide range of treacherous conditions, but the salt of the oceans at least prevents a substantial amount of ice from building up. The stations along the Great Lakes are not so lucky. The combination of high winds, subzero temperatures, and frequent blizzards acting upon sites surrounded by fresh water can lead to terrifying results. Surrounded by towering snowdrifts, entire towers have become encased in ice, impairing their function and imprisoning their keepers inside or preventing them from gaining access. Lake Huron's Spectacle Reef Lighthouse—built after two wrecks occurred on a dangerous reef in 1868—took several years to construct. When keepers arrived to open it for the first time in the spring of 1874, ice had piled more than 30 feet (9.15 m) up the tower; they had to chop it away to reach the door.

OPPOSITE
Heavy clouds roll in toward Heceta Head Lighthouse, which guards the central Oregon coast north of the Siuslaw River.
Florence, Oregon

Intense cold and wild winds combine to produce ice formations of staggering proportions at St. Joseph North Pierhead Light. The utter isolation that often characterized the keeper's existence becomes painfully evident in such scenes. *St. Joseph River, Michigan*

They are ill discoverers that think there is no land,

when they can see nothing but sea.

—*Francis Bacon*

OPPOSITE
Despite the difficulties of building on the site, Spectacle Reef Lighthouse was needed because of the proximity of a dangerous reef deemed by the Lighthouse Board "probably more dreaded by navigators than any other danger now unmarked throughout the entire chain of lakes." *Lake Huron, Michigan*

Minot's Ledge Light is considered the nations most dangerous lighthouse. Improperly constructed, the first Minot's Ledge Lighthouse collapsed into the raging seas in 1851. Two assistant keepers perished along with the tower.

felt in regard to the lighthouse at Minot's Ledge. The weather is still too misty to distinguish if it is still standing." By the next day, it was not—it had tumbled into the sea, leaving only bent iron limbs jutting out of the rock. Two assistant keepers perished along with the tower. Its replacement, completed in 1860, was a conical granite tower that still stands. Because of the one-four-three sequence of its light signal, it has become known as the lovers light, since it seems to flash the message "I-love-you."

The Pacific Coast also has its share of lighthouses that have been prone to natural threats. Set on a rough, sea-swept crag on the northern coast of Oregon, Tillamook Rock Lighthouse rivaled Minot's Ledge hazardous circumstances and proved one of the most difficult lighthouses to build and to access. Even when the furious waters permitted the approach of a boat, the steep rock offered little foothold. Perched on its immense stone roost, the tower soared 150 feet (45.75 m) above

The small building to the right
of Portland Head Light's tower
houses the station's fog signal,
much needed in this region of
frequent fogs. *Portland,
Maine*

*Society is all but rude
To this delicious solitude.*
—Andrew Marvel

The rocky, trecherous coasts of New England were the sights of many shipwrecks, and were a breeding ground for "mooncussers"—pirates who awaited (and perhaps even helped cause) shipwrecks in hopes of looting the valuable cargo.

FOLLOWING PAGE
A storm approaches West Breakwater Lighthouse, just northeast of Cleveland on the shore of Lake Erie. *Fairport, Ohio*

the ocean. Keepers and supplies had to be hoisted up by derrick 75 feet (almost 23 m) onto a concrete landing. After a relentless eighteen months of construction the lantern was lit in 1881, unfortunately four weeks too late to save the twenty men who perished just a mile from Tillamook in a wreck precipitated by a heavy fog. Though the light has since been decommissioned, it served for nearly eighty years under the care of five keepers at all times because of the extreme danger of the site. One keeper even reported green water streaming over the very top of the tower on one occasion; on another he witnessed a storm that created waves strong enough to tear rocks from the island and hurl them through the metal dome of the lantern. Several years later a winter storm propelled stones, seaweed, and fish into the lantern and smashed the lens. Hundred-foot waves regularly pounded the station, whose perilous situation earned it the nickname "the hoodoo light."

DARING RESCUES

Throughout the history of lighthouses, keepers and their assistants have performed many acts of bravery. Nearly every one of them took

This nineteenth-century watercolor depicts a heroic rescue performed an English lighthouse keeper and his daughter. James and Grace Darling rowed their small boat through the heavy seas of a terrible storm to save the passengers and crew of a wrecked ship in 1838.

part in rescue efforts at some point in their careers, venturing in tiny boats on merciless seas. Going above and beyond the call of duty, they saved victims of countless shipwrecks and capsized vessels. Just between the years 1911 and 1921, for example, keepers managed to save more than twelve hundred people. Most of these courageous deeds went relatively unnoticed, but once the Lighthouse Board instituted a program to award acts of bravery, some became recognized and were even publicized monthly in the Bureau of Lighthouses' *Lighthouse Service Bulletin*. Certain keepers received gold medals, silver watches, and other rewards for their heroic acts.

Although most rescues were relatively ordinary, some were terrifying, life-threatening episodes. During a severe winter storm in 1885 around Portland, Maine, Marcus Hanna, keeper of the Cape Elizabeth Lighthouse, rescued two seamen from a schooner that had iced over so badly they had to throw the deckload overboard just to keep the vessel afloat. Before long the schooner seemed destined for destruction and the wave-drenched sailors, now frozen to

Birds surround Lake Michigan's Ile aux Galets Lighthouse. When huge flocks descended en masse, they could do serious damage to lanterns. Keepers tried numerous solutions, including fencing in the glass with wire screens. *Sturgeon Bay, Michigan*

OPPOSITE
As evidenced by this shot of Petoskey Lighthouse, whole towers in the Great Lakes region may become enclosed in ice during severe winters, interfering with lighthouse functions and—before the era of automation—endangering the keepers. *Petoskey, Michigan*

Foghorns

Even in the absence of a storm, fog might present a serious navigational hazard, requiring keepers to tend the fog signals diligently until the air cleared. The first fog signal in the United States was a cannon installed in 1719 at the country's first lighthouse, Boston Light. The first fog signal on the West Coast was also a cannon; obtained from the army, it was at California's Point Bonita in 1855 and manned by a former army sergeant. Just two months later an infamous San Francisco fog settled in, lasting for three days straight and allowing the sergeant only two hour's rest. Within two years, the cannon had been replaced by a fog bell.

Bells had been introduced at several New England lights in the 1820s. At first they were rung by hand to answer passing vessels, but by the 1860s the Lighthouse Board had engines installed to sound them mechanically. Larger bells (weighing as much as 4,000 pounds) were later installed, utilizing striking machinery governed by clockwork to ring regular, recognizable characteristics. But even large bells were not really sufficient for seacoast use. Beginning in 1851, trumpets utilizing compressed air were used experimentally. These proved more penetrating than bells, but were still not entirely satisfactory. Steam whistles were investigated as early as 1855; though powerful, they took time to put it into operation, which presented a problem since fog often descended quickly.

The diaphone, invented by the Canadian Lighthouse service, proved an important innovation. Powered by compressed air, steam, or electricity, it gave a distinct, easily discernible sound. To enable vessels to distinguish locations by sound, each foghorn emits a particular sound and number of blasts. Today's light stations generally employ diaphones, as well as radio beacons, which not only provide navigational assistance in low-visibility periods but enable distant vessels to determine their positions in any weather.

Lightships

Hazardous conditions were not limited to existing lighthouses. Certain regions required light stations to improve navigation, yet presented situations that made construction of a traditional lighthouse unfeasible. Originally called lightboats, lightships were intended to provide navigational aids in the many locations where a lighthouse was impractical. The world's first lightship was launched in the early 1730s in England, where the Medway River joins the Thames. It took nearly a century for one to be anchored in the United States; in 1820, Chesapeake Bay's Willoughby Spit (near Norfolk, Virginia) received the first United States lightship. Six more lightships were activated on bays, rivers, and harbors by 1823. That year also saw the launching of the earliest outside light vessels (those stationed in the ocean), activated around New York Harbor. The first one in New York supplemented the operations of New Jersey's Sandy Hook Lighthouse to mark the main channel leading to the Port of New York. The United States possessed twenty-six active lightships by 1837, and the number increased to forty-two by the time the Lighthouse Board assumed control about fifteen years later.

The lightship is a comparatively recent development in the field of navigation, yet its history was short-lived; the age of the active lightship lasted only about 160 years. The advances made possible by the screwpile light, and later the caisson structure, began the lightship's path toward obsolescence, since these types of lighthouses could be placed on previously impractical marine sites. By the 1960s, technology had enabled the replacement of lightships with stationary platforms similar to those used for offshore oil rigs. Fewer than thirty lightships are still on the water. Many have been converted into floating museums.

Although the lightship no longer sees duty as a navigational aid, it became noteworthy at the turn of the century for a particular occurrence. On August 23, 1899, the very first wireless transmission ever sent by the United States Lighthouse Service was made from one of these vessels, the San Francisco Lightship, to a station on the ocean front of San Francisco.

At the mercy of the raging sea, a British warship is battered as easily as a tiny rowboat. *A First-Rate Man-of-War Driving on a Reef of Rocks, Foundering in a Gale,* a nineteenth-century oil by George Philip Reinagle, captures the sense of raw power unleashed by a fearsome storm.

The fogbound Yaquina Head Lighthouse appears to hover mysteriously between land and sky, the dangerously craggy coast all but obscured in the mist-shrouded air. *Newport, Oregon*

their perches in the rigging, had virtually given up hope. After the keeper's unsuccessful attempts to throw a line aboard, a towering wave dashed the vessel against the rocks. Finally Hanna—eventually aided by neighbors who came to help with the rescue—managed to haul the nearly paralyzed mariners to shore and carry them through the deep snow to the fog signal station. Though the captain had been lost, the two men did survive, thanks to the dedication of Keeper Hanna.

THE CURSE OF THE WRECKERS

Saving the lives of sailors and passengers was actually a secondary consideration in the decision to build a lighthouse. The immediate purpose was to enable safe passage of the ship's cargo, the value of which was often deemed far greater than that of the people on board. In the eyes of the merchants and ship owners, the cost of building a

OPPOSITE
The 51-foot-tall Grand Haven South Pierhead Inner Light guards Lake Michigan's eastern shore on a bleak winter's day as ice encroaches on the catwalk. *Ottawa County, Michigan*

Bird Traffic

Despite the routine nature of many lighthouse-tending duties, unusual events did occur. Attracted by the light, birds often flew into the lantern. The occasional avian visitor presented no problem, but sometimes huge flocks would collide with the lantern, shattering the glass and even breaking the lens prism. Keepers attempted many solutions to protect their lenses, from placing heavy wire screening around the lantern to firing off guns to frighten the birds away to actually shooting them. Resourceful—or desperate—individuals tried a different approach. One November, keepers at the very remote lighthouse on Boon Island found themselves trapped at the station and running out of food. Hearing loud thumps coming from the lantern room, they raced upstairs to discover that eight ducks had crashed into the windows. They were thus able to prepare themselves an unexpected but plentiful Thanksgiving feast.

An Ancient Occupation

Shipwrecks, both accidental and premeditated, are as old as seafaring itself. The ancient Greeks and Romans salvaged shipwreck cargo and sold survivors into slavery. This practice, called "wrecking," was a highly profitable profession along the coasts of Britain for centuries. With its isolated and merciless coastline, Cornwall was a wreckers' paradise. Many in its impoverished population looked to wrecking as a path toward improving their station. It was even said that some vicars in remote Cornish fishing villages encouraged their congregation not necessarily to pray for wrecks, but to urge the Lord that if they had to happen, He help guide them in the right direction.

OPPOSITE
Awash in the glow of sunset, St. Joseph North Pierhead Light guards the river entrance. One of the first lights on Lake Michigan, the station was built in 1832 and enlarged in 1886. *St. Joseph River, Michigan*

PREVIOUS PAGE
Seen at a distance beyond snow-draped dunes, St. Joseph North Pierhead Light juts far out into the icy river. *St. Joseph River, Michigan*

The fog bell of Trinidad Head Lighthouse was replaced by a modern foghorn, but the original bell now stands beside a replica of the lighthouse, built to be more accessible to tourist traffic. *Trinidad, California*

lighthouse was warranted only in relation to the value of the goods. Lights were therefore judged necessary in important trading ports to ensure that goods reached the harbor safely.

But a ship laden with expensive goods made tempting quarry indeed for those on land inclined toward the ways of piracy. Since more shipwrecks meant greater plunder, wreckers resisted all efforts at lighthouse building. Shattered vessels meant food, liquor, precious woods and metals, and costly fabrics free for the taking. Profiting from death and disaster, wreckers despised lighthouses and not only waited for ships to smash upon the rocks but actively sought to lure them there. The jagged coasts and treacherous shoals of New England made the wreckers' efforts that much easier. Lonely and dangerous coastlines were ideal breeding grounds for these land pirates. Wreckers not only fought new lighthouse construction; they may have directed their efforts toward disabling existing lights as well. When fire destroyed several towers in the 1840s, many blamed the wreckers.

The most horrifying aspect of this practice was its active encouragement. Wreckers were often known as "mooncussers" due to their penchant for cursing the light of the moon and praying for dark nights, during which ships were more likely to run aground. Fog and storms were their allies as well. These unscrupulous types built fires or placed signals in dangerous spots to lure unsuspecting vessels onto the rocks. Thinking the light marked a harbor's entrance, a captain would steer his ship toward it, only to realize the deception too late. Dashed upon the rocky shore, the ship and whatever treasures it contained then fell prey to the looters.

To increase their powers of deception, mooncussers might carry a lighted pole across the beach, or attach lanterns to horses or cattle and lead the animals along the shore. To a ship out at sea, such lurching spots of brightness resembled another vessel moving through unobstructed waters. Or a wrecker might stand on a dangerous outcropping swinging a lantern that had been fastened to the end of a broom handle, thus fooling a ship's captain into thinking the light was hanging from a safely anchored vessel. If their evil labors succeeded, the wreckers would scramble swiftly aboard, claiming the ship and its cargo as their own.

OPPOSITE
Point Betsie Lighthouse—
considered an important light
because of its location at a
turning point for several
routes along Lake Michigan—
was the last light tended
by a keeper on the lake's
eastern shore. Severe weather and erosion continue to
threaten the site. *Frankfort,
Michigan*

Fire Island

The fires that were kindled along the shores of New York's Fire Island during the last century may have earned the island its name. The flames were most likely meant to help guide ships through Long Island Sound, but some may also have been lit by wreckers to lure ships to their doom.

So important was this site as a navigational aid that in the 1850s the Lighthouse Board ordered a tall tower built there to replace the 1826 structure. The board declared the resulting 167-foot tower the most important lighthouse for transatlantic steamers, which set their course for this light on voyages from Europe and departed from it for the return trip.

Praise the sea; on shore remain.

—*John Florio*

Lighthouses in Wartime

Mooncussers were not the only ones to interfere with lighthouse functions. In times of war, the control of lighthouses has proven a great advantage. When British troops took over Boston Light at the start of the American Revolution, American troops snuck in and set fire to the structure, first removing the lamps from the lantern. After British attempts to repair it met with further American resistance, the Redcoats blew up the tower as they evacuated Boston, rendering the light useless to American forces. During the Civil War, when the Union navy had command of most lighthouses, the Confederates sought to destroy as many lights as possible, successfully darkening 164 towers on the southern coast. In the Second World War, the United States blacked out more than fourteen hundred lights all along both coasts and kept others dimmed to permit just enough light to steer friendly ships into harbor.

OPPOSITE
Located near Halifax on the peninsula's Atlantic side, Peggy's Cove Lighthouse warns ships off the region's treacherously rocky coasts.
Nova Scotia, Canada

A storm of 1893 left Chandeleur Island Lighthouse canting at a severe angle. Broken bricks from the tower were employed as foundation fill in the replacement tower.
New Orleans, Louisiana

In their opposition to lighthouses, mooncussers railed against the loss of their livelihood. Some believed they were entitled to the spoils, claiming they provided an important service by rescuing shipwreck victims and offering them food and shelter. But many wreckers showed no such mercy. Placing little or no value on human life, they often preferred to leave victims to die—or even to kill them—rather than be allowed to survive and perhaps bring the criminals to justice. As early as the seventeenth century, the colonies had instituted legislation requiring that shipwrecks be reported to the town clerk immediately so that salvage could begin, but it was usually more profitable to stay silent.

Yet these legions of darkness were gradually overcome. The construction of Boston Light—the first lighthouse in the New World—resulted because Boston merchants in 1713 petitioned the General Court for a lighthouse, seeking to put a stop to this thievery. By 1774, Virginia had declared wrecking a crime punishable by death. The Massachusetts Humane Society began building rescue stations in the 1780s to provide food, firewood, and shelter to shipwreck survivors.

Perched on a cliff high above the shore, the Heceta Head Lighthouse ensures a safer passage to vessels navigating the rocky Oregon coast.
Florence, Oregon

CHAPTER FIVE

Lighting the Future

OPPOSITE
At low tide keepers at
Nubble Light (officially
called Cape Neddick
Lighthouse) would walk
to the island. Visitors
used to be allowed to do
the same until officials
deemed the practice
unsafe. *York, Maine*

Erected in 1792, the
first Cape Henry
Lighthouse exhibited
large cracks by 1870,

when the Lighthouse
Board declared it "in
danger of being thrown
down by some heavy
gale." In 1881 this dis-
tinctively patterned tower
was built beside the
first, but the original
remains standing to this
day. *Virginia Beach,
Virginia*

The arrival of automation came at the turn of the century. The first lighthouse powered by electricity was northern New Jersey's Navesink Light, where an electric arc bivalve lens was installed in 1898. The Lighthouse Board began testing electricity for general lighthouse use around 1900, but the majority of United States lighthouses were not converted to electricity until the 1920s and 1930s because they were located at great distance from power lines. The introduction of electricity gradually resulted in the automation of virtually all lighthouses, eliminating the need for resident keepers.

Quite a few modern lighthouses are vastly different structures from the traditional lighthouse. With today's technology, what was once an elaborate station complete with tower, dwellings, and workshops has been reduced to a simple platform or post that provides everything necessary to operate the streamlined lenses and self-contained lights now in use, lights that turn themselves on right before sunset and wink

The Lighthouse was then a silvery, misty-looking tower with a yellow eye, that opened suddenly, and softly in the evening.

Virginia Woolf, To the Lighthouse

LEFT
A patriotic folk art piece by contemporary Vermont artist Warren Kimble testifies to the continued popularity of the lighthouse.

OPPOSITE
Breathtakingly sited at the edge of the Kilauea Point National Wildlife Refuge, Kilauea Point Lighthouse was the last Hawaiian light station to retain its keeping staff. *Kauai, Hawaii*

NEXT PAGE
The Boston Lighthouse is the only operational lighthouse that is still manned by a full staff. While other lighthouses have become automated, an act of Congress mandates that this historic station retain its staff as a tribute to lighthouse keepers. *Boston, Massachusetts*

off just after the sun rises. Technological advances have drastically reduced the size of lights and lenses and made them weatherproof. Coupled with other mechanization, such as radio beacons and radar, such smaller, lighter apparatus needs only a basic setup for efficient operation. Where once a whole family might be needed to keep a station running smoothly, nowadays a lighthouse generally requires human attention only about four times a year. Contemporary keepers—all members of the Coast Guard—are known as ANTs, short for Aid to Navigation Teams.

Although Fresnel lenses are still used in a number of lighthouses, Coast Guard personnel have installed a new system of automation known as ATON, which employs plastic lenses styled after the Fresnel design. The lenses contain six or more small bulbs on a belt; when a bulb burns out, the belt moves another one into place. In many locations, solar panels have been installed to recharge the lights' batteries.

Fewer than sixty stations retained their keepers by the late 1960s; today, keepers are virtually a relic of the past. The United States Coast Guard—the current administrator of the country's lighthouses—set out in 1989 to complete its plan to automate all lights under its command. Although the Coast Guard did not initiate automation (it was begun by the Bureau of Lighthouses), it has done the most in instituting this economical process. The only fully staffed lighthouse still in operation is the one at Boston Harbor. Originally scheduled for

Going Electric

Surprisingly, the very first use of electricity in a lighthouse capacity did not occur in a lighthouse. When an electric arc was installed in the Statue of Liberty in 1886, it became the first electrified structure to serve as a lighthouse. Now a national monument, the statue is no longer considered a navigational aid, but for a brief time the lady and her torch did help to guide ships into New York Harbor.

One of the most charming light stations in the country, Cape Neddick (Nubble) Lighthouse glows in the pink radiance of sunrise. *York, Maine*

OPPOSITE
The Little Red Lighthouse is dwarfed by its immense neighbor, the George Washington Bridge. Saved from demolition by fame acquired through a popular children's book, the lighthouse is now officially part of Fort Washington Park. *New York, New York*

Its tower irreparably damaged and lens destroyed by the 1906 earthquake, Point Arena Lighthouse was rebuilt two years later as a 155-foot cylindrical tower of reinforced concrete. The fog signal building contains a small museum. *Point Arena, California*

automation, this station—the first lighthouse in the country—is required by an act of Congress to retain its staff to memorialize its historic significance and as a tribute to the significance of the lighthouse keeper.

PRESERVING THE LIGHTS

Nowadays, only about seven hundred to eight hundred traditional lighthouses remain, fewer than two-thirds of which still see active service. In past decades, obsolete stations often ended up in private control, sometimes sold at public auction. Today many inactive lights are administered by the National Park Service and the United States Forest Service. A number of them are centerpieces of state or national parks, or have been converted into maritime museums or tourist attractions filled with lighthouse artifacts. Others have been leased and restored

We are as near to heaven by sea as by land!

—Sir Humphrey Gilbert

Nubble Light

One of the country's most picturesque lights is southern Maine's Cape Neddick Lighthouse, generally referred to as Nubble Light because the little island on which it stands is known as a nubble. Situated near a popular resort, the station received considerable national television coverage several years ago when the original 1879 tower underwent automation. Each year the town of York celebrates the holidays by decking its beloved lighthouse in thousands of Christmas lights.

by local historical groups, which often take action to preserve the traditional look of a light station after automation. Sometimes the keepers' quarters are restored to their original appearance to provide visitors with a glimpse of the keepers' lifestyle. Some lighthouses have even been transformed into elegant bed-and-breakfast accommodations, or into inexpensive youth hostels for those on a more limited budget.

Many lighthouses are the unfortunate victims of severe erosion. In the past, numerous lights were moved to prevent their destruction, not

to save the towers for their own inherent value but to retain their original purpose of navigational assistance. Today preservation efforts are underway to save lighthouses for historical and cultural reasons. Cape Hatteras Lighthouse—now part of the Cape Hatteras National Seashore and one of the most popular lights in the country—is drastically threatened by erosion. Through the years, teams of experts proposed many solutions to stave off the tower's destruction, including placement of sandbags, constructing a revetment around the tower, replenishing the sand, or moving the tower.

A panoramic view in glowing pastels provides a glorious backdrop for Peggy's Cove Lighthouse, with its vivid red lantern and bright green light. *Nova Scotia, Canada*

That dolphin-torn, that gong-tormented sea.

—William Butler Yeats

Disactivated in 1939, Coquille River Lighthouse had deteriorated badly by the 1970s. The station has since been restored and is open to the public during the summer. *Bandon, Oregon*

Another light that has felt the effects of erosion is Cape Cod's Highland Light, generally the first one sighted by vessels bound from Europe to Massachusetts Bay. First lit in 1798, the tower was rebuilt in 1833 and again in 1857. In his mid-nineteenth-century book *Cape Cod*, Henry David Thoreau expressed concern that the tower would soon topple as a result of the steadily encroaching sea. In its earliest days the light stood 510 feet (155.5 m) from the edge of the Truro Bluffs; in 1995 that distance had shrunk to less than 125 feet (38.12 m). In the summer of 1996, the 650-ton lighthouse was successfully moved about 450 feet (137 m) to a safer location.

OPPOSITE
The original 1801 tower of Annisquam Harbor Lighthouse was replaced in 1897 with this 41-foot cylinder. The flashing white light was electrified in 1972. *Annisquam, Massachusetts*

A number of lighthouse preservation associations have sprung up throughout the country. The Lighthouse Preservation Society in Rockport, Massachusetts, and the United States Lighthouse Society in San Francisco are particularly active in preservation efforts, along with the National Trust for Historic Preservation and other federal organizations. Celebrities occasionally use their drawing power to stage benefit performances or create works of art for sale as fundraisers to aid in saving the lighthouses.

On the Road

To salute the charms of the lighthouse, and perhaps to increase awareness of the movement to preserve the lights, several states feature the structure on their license plates. North Carolina's first historical attraction license plate depicts the Cape Hatteras Lighthouse. Connecticut, Massachusetts, New Jersey, New York, Ohio, and Pennsylvania also offer lighthouse plates.

Little Red

The Little Red Lighthouse is the only tower ever to be saved due to the fame it acquired as the subject of a children's book. Originally part of the Sandy Hook Range Lights and known as North Hook light, it was dismantled in 1917 to remove it from the line of fire of coastal artillery guns. Reassembled and re-lit in 1921 as the Jeffrey's Hook Lighthouse, it guarded the Hudson River for several years as the first lighthouse encountered by those journeying up the river. But once the George Washington Bridge was constructed in 1931, the bridge light guided river traffic, rendering the lighthouse obsolete.

Slated for removal in 1951, the tower's fate took a turn that administrators had not reckoned on. Thousands of children, who had come to love the structure through the book *The Little Red Lighthouse and the Great Gray Bridge*, flooded the Coast Guard with letters pleading that the lighthouse be saved. The organization obliged by granting it to the City of New York, which made it a part of Fort Washington Park. Since the early 1990s, the Urban Park Rangers of New York have sponsored an annual family festival to gain attention and resources to maintain this landmark lighthouse.

Destroyed by a storm in 1984,
Great Point Lighthouse was
replicated in 1987, complete
with a solar-powered cofferdam
to protect it from future erosion.
Nantucket, Massachusetts

Perched on a bluff severely threatened by erosion, Southeast Lighthouse is endangered by the encroaching sea. Plans are underway to move the station to a safer spot. *Block Island, Rhode Island*

LIGHTHOUSE CULTURE

Emblematic of selfless dedication and poetic isolation, lighthouses are a popular motif in today's culture. Countless collectible items feature lighthouse themes, and seven states have placed lighthouses on their license plates. Organizations as diverse as a major insurance company and the eponymous association for the blind have chosen the lighthouse as a corporate logo, based its symbolic power as a beacon to illuminate the darkness. Literature has turned to the lighthouse as an extension of the concept of the ivory tower: a symbol of the timeless yearning to retreat from life's daily urgency, to abide in a tranquil setting removed from everyday cares. No matter that the reality of the keeper's existence was often far from peaceful and comprised an endless round of daily tasks; the modern imagination has idealized lighthouse living and proclaimed it sublime.

Technology has drastically changed the age-old traditions under which lighthouses operated, but it has certainly not diminished the charm these structures continue to exude, nor the fervor invested by many in efforts to preserve and maintain them, nor the power they continue to hold over the imagination. And technology has had another sort of ramification on lighthouse lore, one that no engineer, administrator, or keeper of the traditional tower could have anticipated in the heyday of the lighthouse: the impact of the Internet. There are now literally thousands of electronic sites devoted to lighthouses, covering everything from serious historical, architectural studies (complete with full-color pictures) to urgent preservation efforts; from geographical surveys of the world's lights to individuals' personal preferences about the greatest towers; from book stores and gift shops hawking lighthouse-related items to hobbyists who create lighthouse-themed crafts.

So You Want to Be a Lighthouse Keeper

According to a list originally compiled by the United States Lighthouse Society in San Francisco, there are nineteen lighthouses around the country offering guest accommodations. Most of these range from bed-and-breakfast establishments resembling country inns to simple youth hostel setups. But the New Dungeness Light Station in Sequim, Washington, gives visitors first-hand experience at tending a lighthouse. Established in 1857 and overhauled in 1927, the station stands on a remote sand-spit in the Straits of Juan de Fuca. The light is staffed entirely by volunteers, twenty-four hours a day, year round. Each Friday or Saturday, a new team of two couples arrives (sometimes with children), to spend the week living at the furnished keeper's quarters (built in 1904). For their week's tour of duty they are assigned specific tasks to maintain the house and grounds, and, of course, to keep the light burning.

Yaquina Head Lighthouse was originally known as Cape Foulweather Light because the building materials were inadvertantly landed at this spot in 1873, rather than at their intended destination of Cape Foulweather, four miles to the north. *Newport, Oregon*

The slender hexagonal tower
of San Felipe Lighthouse
soars above the landscape.
Baja, California

Despite the relentless commercialism evident in much of today's lighthouse paraphernalia, the very fact that the lighthouse still enjoys such vast popularity surely goes a long way in the efforts to preserve them. It also appears to reflect a certain reverence for tradition and symbol that many still hold dear in an increasingly modernized world. In his introduction to *Lighthouses of the Maine Coast and the Men Who Keep Them*, Robert Coffin elegantly defines the poetry of the lighthouse: "Our lighthouses are more than mere guides to mariners . . . more than mere havens of peace. They are close to the things that count most with a poet. Close to the patterns of the tide and the passing of hours, sunrise, sunset, night. Close to solitude from which the best music comes. Close to storms and birds on the wing—patterns of a life that does not change, designs in the everlasting things." In humanity's quest for a symbol of steadfastness with universal appeal, a glimmer of permanence in an ephemeral age, evidence that something made by humankind can withstand the tests of nature and of time, the lighthouse stands as the perfect symbol.

OPPOSITE
With its distinctive black-and-white swirl, Cape Hatteras Lighthouse is one of the most widely recognized towers and serves as the state symbol of North Carolina.
Buxton, North Carolina

Lighthouse Collectibles

Not only do fans of lighthouses make it a point to visit as many lighthouses as possible on their travels around the country, but they buy anything and everything related to their favorite subject. Appearing on everything from T-shirts to blankets, housewares to coffee mugs, nightlights to Christmas ornaments, lighthouses manifest themselves over all manner of collectible items. Lighthouse buffs are so numerous that one business thrives entirely on this theme. The Lighthouse Depot in Wells, Maine—self-billed as "the world's largest lighthouse gift and collectible store"—devotes itself exclusively to merchandise featuring lighthouses.

INDEX